catch you later!

So, trainee, you've learned some great new **counterintelligence tradecraft**! You've used invisible **spy dust** to find out who's been snooping around your headquarters, you've lifted fingerprints, you've marked money, and you've caught a spy's radio waves.

And don't forget the code you broke in Operation . Here's another message for you to decode, as your final counterintelligence challenge!

So, figure out the message, and we'll see you next month!

the answer spot

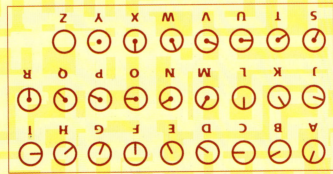

Pages 35–36 (Operation Catch the Wave):
Part 1: a. Home
b. The bus stop
c. The ice cream store
d. The mailbox

Page 42 (Operation 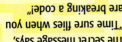):
The secret message is in clock code. The clock code uses a circle with a line that represents the hour hand and, for letters, the hour hand and the minute hand.
Part 2: The spy is in the park!
More from Headquarters: The spy is at the school!

Page 26 (Operation Read My Lips):
Carlos is the mole.

Page 48 (Catch You Later!):
The secret message says, "Time sure flies when you are breaking a code!" "It takes time to catch a spy!"

came right after Ames's lunch meetings with a Russian contact.

At this point, the mole hunters were confident they had their man, so they turned the case over to the FBI. (Since the CIA can't make arrests, it has to work with the FBI on spy cases like Ames's. The FBI handles law enforcement, like a police force, so it *can* make arrests.)

The FBI opened its case on Ames on May 12, 1993, code-naming the case "Nightmover." As part of their investigation, FBI agents set up **surveillance** on Ames at home and at work. They started monitoring Ames's phone conversations with his wife. They even snatched the trash cans from Ames's driveway in the middle of the night and replaced the cans with identical ones. When they searched Ames's trash, the FBI agents found a torn Post-it note with a message to the Russians written on it.

When the FBI had gathered enough evidence to make an arrest, they surrounded Ames's red Jaguar as he drove it to CIA headquarters on February 21, 1994. Stepping out of the car, Ames said, "There must be some mistake."

He looked flabbergasted as he was being handcuffed. "You've got to be kidding," he said. But he soon realized this was no joke.

Since Ames's phone conversations with his wife had revealed Rosario's support of her husband's spying, Rosario was arrested as well. The FBI then searched Ames's home, discovering all kinds of documents, letters, and computer disks that proved Ames's **espionage**.

Ames pleaded guilty to charges of espionage

Ames and his wife, Rosario, after being arrested by the FBI.

and accepted a sentence of life in prison without the possibility of parole. He cooperated with the CIA and FBI in return for a sentence of five years for Rosario so she could be with their son. She was deported to her native Colombia after her release in 1999.

So, in the end, Ames paid the price for selling the CIA's secrets, but his country and the Russian agents he betrayed paid much more dearly. As they say, "money talks," and in the case of Aldrich Ames, money spoke loudly. Ames couldn't resist the temptation of a life of luxury, even though he knew it would cost people's lives and his country's security. He was even bold enough to drive his luxury car, bought with cash he'd made from selling CIA secrets, right into the CIA's parking lot. It's a good thing that the CIA's mole hunters saw the signs—and drove that mole out.

The Spy's Guide to Counter-intelligence

BY **Jim Wiese** WITH **H. Keith Melton**
SPY EXPERT

SCHOLASTIC INC.

NEW YORK TORONTO LONDON AUCKLAND SYDNEY
MEXICO CITY NEW DELHI HONG KONG BUENOS AIRES

UV light

In order to "trap" suspected spies, CIA counterspies would brush invisible powder on a folder containing supposed "secret information," and they'd leave the folder where it would be accessible to suspected spies. The person who picked up the folder would leave a fingerprint that would glow under UV light.

ISBN 0-439-33646-5
Copyright © 2003 by Scholastic Inc.

Editor: Andrea Menotti
Designers: Robert Rath, Lee Kaplan
Illustrations: Daniel Aycock
Photos: www.spyimages.net

All rights reserved. Published by Scholastic Inc. No part of this publication may be reproduced, stored in a retrieval system, or transmitted in any form or by any means, electronic, mechanical, photocopying, recording, or otherwise, without the prior written permission of the publisher. For information regarding permission, write to Scholastic Inc., Attention: Permissions Department, 557 Broadway, New York, NY 10012.

SCHOLASTIC, SPY UNIVERSITY, and associated logos are trademarks and/or registered trademarks of Scholastic Inc.

12 11 10 9 8 7 6 5 4 3 2 1   3 4 5 6 7 8/0

Printed in the U.S.A.

First Scholastic printing, April 2003

The publisher has made every effort to ensure that the activities in this book are safe when done as instructed. Children are encouraged to do their spy activities with willing friends and family members and to respect others' right to privacy. Adults should provide guidance and supervision whenever the activity requires.

TABLE OF Contents

Hot on the Trail!	Page 4
About This Month's Spy Gear 👓	Page 6
About This Month's Web Site (and the Password Spot) 🖥️	Page 6
Spy Talk	Page 7
Spy Quest: Catch the Mole!	Page 8
Spy Missions:	
#1: Operation Ultra Dust 👓 🖥️	Page 10
#2: Operation Glow-Getter 👓	Page 14
#3: Operation Money Marker 👓	Page 17
#4: Operation Spy Print 👓 🖥️	Page 19
#5: Operation Read My Lips 👓	Page 24
#6: Operation Ink Link	Page 28
#7: Operation Bug Plant	Page 31
#8: Operation Catch the Wave	Page 34
#9: Operation Spies on Wheels	Page 37
#10: Operation 🖥️	Page 42
Spy Feature: Aldrich Ames, CIA Mole	Page 44
Catch You Later!	Page 48
The Answer Spot	Page 48

👓 **This means you'll use your Spy Gear in this activity.**

🖥️ **This means you can find a related activity on the Spy University web site.**

Hot on the

Imagine this: It's Saturday morning and you get a call from your friend Jeff, a member of your **spy network**. Jeff says, "I can't do my homework. Can you come over and explain it to me?" Shaken, you say "yes" and hang up the phone. Something serious has happened. Jeff has just told you in code that a secret message has been snatched by a spy. And, as a **counterintelligence** expert, it's your job to track down the culprit!

If you're wondering just how you're going to do that, have no fear. This month's training is all about catching spies. You've learned how to *be* a spy, but now's your chance to see what it's like to play for the *other* team—the **counterspies**! You'll learn how to set **traps** for spies with glow-in-the-dark dust, how to lift a spy's fingerprints from a glass, and even how to follow spies on wheels! After your counterintelligence training, you'll have all the skills you'll need to nab even the sneakiest spies. So, grab your spy-catcher's net, and let's get on the trail!

What Is Counterintelligence?

Counter means "against" and *intelligence* is "the act of gathering information," so counterintelligence is working *against* an enemy spy who's trying to *gather information* about you, your spy agency, or your country. Counterintelligence might involve tracking down foreign spies, or it might mean rooting out **moles** or **double agents** who are pretending to be on your side but are secretly working for the enemy. In short, counterintelligence (known as "CI" in the spy world) is spying on spies and stopping them from spying on you.

What's a Counterspy?

A **counterspy** is a counterintelligence officer (the word "counterspy" is just a lot easier on the ear!). Counterspies are specially trained to catch moles and enemy spies by gathering evidence that shows they've been spying. In this way, counterspies are like detectives, since they rely on many of

TRAIL!

the same techniques that detectives use to solve crimes. Counterspies are also like guards protecting the security of information, personnel, and equipment.

Where Do Counterspies Work?

In the United States, the FBI is in charge of catching spies who operate within the country. The CIA also has its own counterintelligence division that focuses on finding moles and double agents.

In the United Kingdom, counterintelligence is handled by MI5 (which stands for Military Intelligence 5, but the agency is officially called the Security Service). In Russia, it's the Federal Security Service (FSB). Check out the Spy Map on the Spy University web site (**www.scholastic.com/spy**) to find out about other counterintelligence services around the world.

FBI Special Surveillance Group patch (above).

The crest of the FSB, the Russian counter-intelligence service (left).

What Techniques Do Counterspies Use?

Counterspies use all kinds of techniques to observe and trace a spy's activities. Here are a few:

- **Surveillance:** This can mean taking pictures of a suspected spy with a hidden camera, planting listening devices called **bugs**, or even following a spy as he moves around town.

  - **Forensic science:** Counterspies can use science to link a spy to an act of **espionage**. Forensic techniques include fingerprint analysis, lip print analysis, comparing hair and cloth fibers, and DNA testing.

  - **Traps:** Spies might use a special invisible **spy dust** to track the movements of anyone who touches it.

So, counterspy, are you ready to learn this month's **tradecraft** and catch some spies?

ABOUT THIS MONTH'S SPY GEAR

Counterintelligence is always easier if you've got the right stuff. So, you've been issued some very special Spy Gear to carry out this month's operations. You've got:

- **An Ultraviolet (UV) light.** You can use this light to detect ink from your UV marker (see below) and the glow of UV spy dust (also see below).

- **A UV marker.** The markings are invisible in normal light, but when you shine your UV light on them, the writing glows!

- **UV spy dust.** This isn't ordinary dust—it glows green under UV light! You can sprinkle it on any surface, and then you can tell if someone touched the surface by shining the UV light on the suspect's hands. Your suspect will also leave a trail of dust on other objects he touches!

- **A brush.** Use this to apply your UV spy dust.

- **A magnifying glass.** Like a detective, you can use this to examine fingerprints, lip prints, and other traces left behind by spies!

ABOUT THIS MONTH'S WEB SITE

You now have access to the counterintelligence session on the Spy University web site at **www.scholastic.com/spy**. It's got all kinds of spy-catching games to challenge you, so log on soon!

the password spot

Shhhh. This month's web site password: **spycatch**

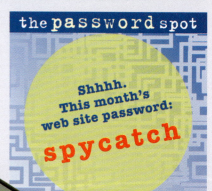

This small, portable, battery-powered UV light source is used by Russian counterspies.

SPY TALK

Before you go too far, you'll need to get acquainted with a few counterintelligence terms. Go over them before you start the operations! You'll see these words in **boldface** throughout the book.

▼ **Bug:** A miniature listening device that can transmit conversations taking place in a room (or on a telephone) to a receiver at another location.

▼ **Cheiloscopy:** The study of lip prints. (Pronounced KYE-lah-skuh-pee.)

▼ **Chromatography:** The separation of a chemical mixture (like ink) into its components.

▼ **Cipher:** A form of code in which the letters of a message are replaced with a new set of letters or numbers according to some rule.

▼ **Counterintelligence:** The protection of information, people, and equipment from spies.

▼ **Counterspy:** Someone who works in counterintelligence, investigating and catching spies.

▼ **Criminalist:** A highly trained counterspy.

▼ **Dead drop:** A secret location used for the transfer of materials between a spy and a handler.

▼ **Defect:** To leave the control of one country or intelligence service to serve another country.

▼ **Double agent:** An agent who is recruited by another country's intelligence agency to work secretly against his original agency.

▼ **Espionage:** The field of spying.

▼ **Fluorescence:** The ability of some substances, like your UV spy dust and UV marker, to glow when a special light is shined on them.

▼ **Forensic science:** Scientific techniques used in criminal investigations.

▼ **Handler:** The intelligence officer who manages a spy's work.

▼ **Latent fingerprint:** A fingerprint left on a surface by an oily or dirty finger.

▼ **Mole:** An employee of an intelligence service who secretly works for another country's intelligence service.

▼ **Phosphorescence:** When a substance continues to glow after exposure to light.

▼ **Quick plant:** A technique in which a concealed bug (disguised as a pen, for example) is left behind during a visit to a target's home or office.

▼ **Secret writing:** Techniques used to hide messages.

▼ **Spy dust:** An invisible powder that counterspies use to trace the movements of a spy (by sprinkling the powder on a surface that the spy touches or steps on). Counterspies can later detect the powder on surfaces that the spy handled or walked on.

▼ **Spy network:** A group of spies who work together toward a common goal.

▼ **Surveillance:** The close observation of someone or something (includes watching and listening).

▼ **Target:** The object of surveillance.

▼ **Trace evidence:** Hair, cloth fibers, dirt particles, or any small clues left behind at the scene of a crime.

▼ **Tradecraft:** The special techniques and procedures that spies use to do their work.

▼ **Trapping:** A technique counterspies can use to determine if materials have been touched or if a room has been entered by a spy.

▼ **Triangulation:** A method of using angles from two known locations to pinpoint a third location.

Catch the Mole!

SPYquest The bell rings to start lunch and everyone races out of the classroom. It's Wednesday, and everyone knows that the school newspaper will be distributed at lunch today.

You grab a copy of the newspaper and take it, along with your lunch, to a shaded area in the school's courtyard. You open to the "Around School" gossip column to find out the latest rumors. There's not much of interest in there this week, except:

Is romance in the air for B.C.H. and S.L.L.? We'll have to see how this develops. More later.

You're starting to wonder who B.C.H. is when you feel a tap on your shoulder. It's your friend Beth Harper.

"I see you're reading the 'Around School' column," she says.

"Yeah," you reply. "It's always interesting."

"Well," Beth says, looking around. "In case you haven't guessed, I'm B.C.H., and I want to find out who put that information about me in the paper. I thought you might be able to help, being a spy expert and all."

"Who's S.L.L.?" you ask. "Is it Steven Lowe?"

"Maybe it is, maybe it isn't," she says. "But just between you and me, I *did* write something about S.L.L. in my diary. I think one of my friends read my diary and gave the information to the paper. Will you help me figure out who did it?"

You hesitate a little because a lot of Beth's friends are also *your* friends, and it wouldn't be nice to spy on them. But then again, you're really curious about how this information leaked out, so you tell Beth you'll help her find the "mole" among her friends.

As you think through your options, you decide there are two things you could do to start. First, you could check Beth's diary for fingerprints. Maybe the culprit left one behind. Or, you could go to the school newspaper and see if they'll tell you who provided the information.

- If you decide to check the diary for fingerprints, turn to **page 23**.
- If you decide to talk to some kids at the school newspaper, turn to **page 30**.

This is your Spy Quest for this month. There's only one way to solve it, so choose your path wisely! If you hit a dead end, you'll have to back up and choose another path!

#1 OPERATION ULTRA DUST

SPYmissions

When you've got a **mole** in your **spy network**, what do you do? You **trap** him, of course. But what kind of trap do you use? A net? A snare? Nothing so obvious! Instead, you'll need something *ultra*-sneaky and *ultra*-slick—you'll need some glowing *ultra*violet **spy dust**! This dust is almost invisible in normal light, but when you shine a UV light on it, it glows a ghostly green. This first operation will show you how UV spy dust can help you catch a spy red-handed—or in this case, *green*-handed!

Stuff You'll Need
- File folder
- Markers
- Paper
- Pencils
- 👓 Brush
- 👓 UV spy dust
- 👓 UV light

Your Network
- Several friends to take part in your spy-catching game

What You Do

Part 1: Dust Buster!

In this part of the operation, you'll catch a spy by making his hands glow in the dark!

1 Use a red marker to design a Top Secret file folder.

2 Place several sheets of paper inside the folder. On one of the sheets, write a pretend "security code number," like 257. It doesn't matter what number you write—the point is simply to give your friend something to look for.

3 Use your brush to put a small amount of UV spy dust on the paper with the security code number. Then close the file folder,

TOP SECRET

Warning: Special Clearance Required

The Secret Security Code Number is 257

and brush more UV spy dust on the outside of the file folder. Make sure to cover all the edges so that anyone who touches the folder will get dust on both hands. The dust coating should be almost invisible.

4 Place the file folder on your desk and wash your hands.

5 Invite several friends into your room. Tell them that when you leave the room, one of them will play the role of a spy: He'll take the file folder that's on your desk and look through the papers to find a security code number. After the spy has found the number, he should put the folder back on the desk in its original position. The identity of the spy should be kept secret from you.

6 Leave the room while your friends decide who will be the spy. Then, once the spy has done what he's supposed to do, your friends should call you back into the room.

7 Return to the room and announce that you're going to determine the identity of the spy.

8 Turn off the lights in the room and shine the UV light on each person's hands. Do you see glowing green specks on one person's hand (or hands)? That's your spy!

Note: The dust will continue to glow in the dark after you turn off the UV light. Sometimes that's when it's easiest to see the glow (if the room is *really* dark).

PART 2: DUSTY TRAIL

Does your green-handed spy leave traces of glowing dust on everything he touches? Try this part of the operation to find out!

1 Follow steps 1 through 7 of Part 1, but this time, when you return to the room, hand each friend a piece of paper and a pencil. Have each person sign his or her name on the paper.

2 Collect the papers, being careful to keep them separate. Take them to a dark room or closet while your friends wait.

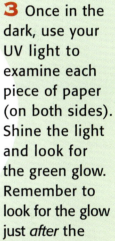

3 Once in the dark, use your UV light to examine each piece of paper (on both sides). Shine the light and look for the green glow. Remember to look for the glow just *after* the light goes out, too. Once you find the paper that has some glowing dust on it, the signature on the paper will identify the spy!

4 Reenter the room and catch your spy!

SPYtales

Over the years, counterspies have developed a variety of spy dusts to help them track and trap spies. Russian counterintelligence officers used nitrophenyl pentadien (NPPD) and luminol. The Russians would place NPPD on doorknobs and on car steering wheels to trace the movements of American officials. An unsuspecting official would touch the doorknob or steering wheel and get the NPPD on his hands. If he later entered an apartment building or an office to meet a contact, he would leave traces of the chemical on the next objects he touched, like the doorknob to his contact's office. All the Russians had to do was use a UV light to find out which room the American official had entered.

This is a jar of nitrophenyl pentadien (NPPD), a kind of spy dust used by Russian counterspies during the 1980s. Even though the dust is brown, when it's lightly dusted on a surface with a brush, it is invisible.

MORE FROM HEADQUARTERS

1 Put the UV spy dust on the doorknob to your headquarters while you're out. If anyone enters while you're away, your UV light will tell you who it was. Just shine the light on the hands of all possible suspects, and (as long as your intruder's hands haven't been washed) you'll figure out whodunit!

Note: If you spread the dust carefully, you'll be able to see if it was disturbed. Just shine the UV light on the knob and look for places where the dust coating is smeared. Even if you don't know who touched the knob, you'll know to step up your security!

2 You can also brush some UV spy dust on the floor in front of the door to your HQ. If someone has entered the room in your absence, you should be able to find tell-tale traces of glowing dust on the soles of the intruder's shoes!

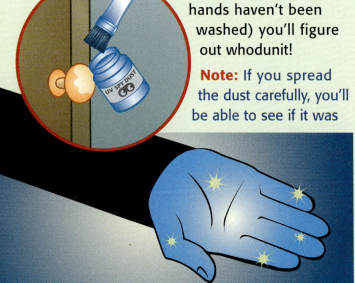

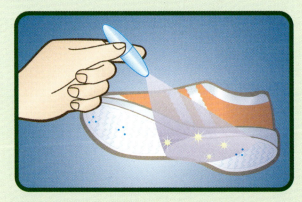

Note: You can also check for footprints on the dust-coated floor by shining your UV light on the dusted area!

3 Stop by the Spy University web site (**www.scholastic.com/spy**) to follow the spy-dusty trail of a suspected spy! Use UV light to figure out where the spy went and what he touched!

WHAT'S THE SECRET?

In case you're curious why the spy dust glows, here's the science behind it. Light energy travels as a wave. The distance from the top of one wave to the top of the following wave is called a wavelength. Humans can only see a specific range of wavelengths. The light that human eyes can detect is called visible light.

Ultraviolet (or UV) light has a wavelength that's smaller than the eye can detect. But, when UV light hits certain substances, such as your UV spy dust, the powder absorbs the UV light and gives off a wavelength that we can see. This is a process called **fluorescence**.

The UV powder will also **phosphoresce**, or *continue* to glow after the UV light is turned off.

A word to wise spies

To make your spy dust *glow away*, wipe the dusted surface with a damp cloth and wash your hands!

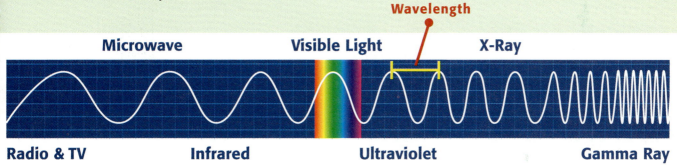

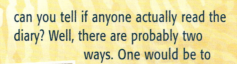

(continued from page 33)

If you're going to trap the mole among Beth's friends, you'll need a plan. You decide to invite Erica and Cassie to Beth's house. You figure you can start a game of hide-and-seek. That will give your suspects a chance to be alone in Beth's room. But how can you tell if anyone actually read the diary? Well, there are probably two ways. One would be to put some UV dust on the diary, then check people's hands later. The other way to trap the culprit would be to use UV dust to coat the floor around the drawer where Beth keeps the diary. Then you can see whose shoes glow under your UV light.

- If you decide to use the UV dust on the diary, turn to **page 43**.
- If you decide to use the UV dust on the floor, turn to **page 32**.

#2 OPERATION GLOW-GETTER

As you learned in your *Trainee Handbook*, invisible ink writing (known in the spy world as **secret writing**) can hide in all kinds of sneaky places. As a **counterspy**, you'll need to know where to look so you can reveal a spy's secret communications. Do you think you have what it takes to spot secret writing in a pile of papers on a spy's desk? Let's find out!

Stuff You'll Need
- Several books, magazines, old letters, and envelopes
- Paper
- UV marker
- Timer or clock
- UV light

Your Network
- A friend to write invisible messages

Invisible ink message

A postcard with invisible ink writing revealed in the corner.

What You Do

1 Invite your friend into your headquarters. Explain that you will be playing a game to test your skills at spotting secret writing.

2 On your desk, place a small pile of items where your friend can write secret messages. You might include a book (*this book, if you want!*), a magazine, a small

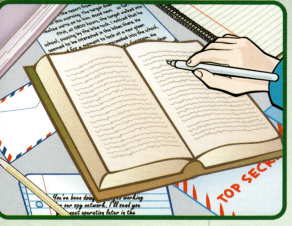

section of a newspaper, or several envelopes with old letters inside. You can use as many or as few items as you want, but remember, the more items you have, the harder your search will be!

3 Tell your friend that when you are out of the room, he should use the UV marker to write five messages on the items on your desk. He should be as sneaky as possible, and he should keep track of exactly where he put each message by making a list of their locations on a sheet of paper.

4 When you return, you will have five minutes to find as many messages as you can. How many can you reveal?

5 After the five minutes are up, ask your friend to show you any messages you didn't find. Why do you think those messages escaped your notice?

6 Gather a new set of materials and try the game again! See if you can get better and better at finding your friend's hiding places.

MORE FROM HEADQUARTERS

Now it's your friend's turn to play the counterspy. Using a new set of materials, hide five messages for your friend to detect with the UV light. Can your friend find more messages than you did? Find out who's the real *glow-getter*!

WHAT'S THE SECRET?

Invisible ink is *invisible*, of course, but spies are still careful and crafty about where they use it. The best spots to hide invisible ink messages are the unusual ones. The message could be on the outside edges of a book, on the inside of the book's cover, or even on the underside of the book's jacket. A message could also hide under the flap of an envelope!

SPYtales

Invisible ink isn't just for spies. Here's one way a political leader used it to catch a critic!

During the 1970s and 80s, Erich Honecker was the head of the Communist party and the East German government (this was when Germany was split into two countries, East Germany and West Germany). Naturally, he had his name and picture in East German newspapers quite often. In 1981, Honecker's office started to receive his photo cut out of the newspaper with the words "is a pig" written over it.

This continued for several months, and it made Honecker *furious*. He set his internal security force (the STASI) to the task of identifying the culprit. They soon narrowed the source down to one town from which the letters were regularly postmarked. When the next newspaper with Honecker's photo appeared, the STASI had taken special precautions. On the back of Honecker's photo in each of the newspapers, the STASI had stamped a unique number using invisible ink. They then recorded where each newspaper was delivered. Sure enough, Honecker received another one of his photos with its rude message. When the STASI turned the photo over and developed the invisible ink, they discovered who was sending the messages. It was the head of the town's Communist party! It isn't known what action the STASI took, but this story probably didn't have a happy ending!

Hidden number 11211

This portable kit allowed CIA officers to set traps for enemy spies and suspected moles. The markers and powders glow under UV light, just like yours.

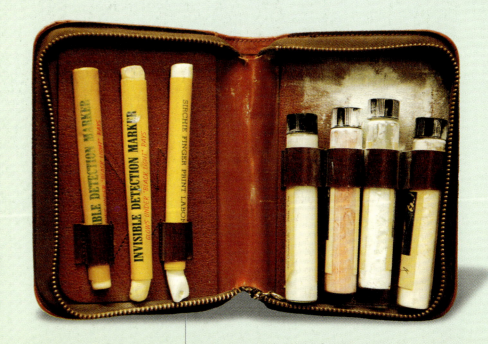

16

#3 OPERATION MONEY Marker

Money makes the world go 'round, they say. It also motivates some people to become traitors and spy against their own countries, as you'll find out when you read this month's **Spy Feature** (on page 44).

This operation will show you one way to use that desire for money to catch a spy. With your UV marker, you can make secret marks on a dollar bill, and you can use those marks to discover who's getting paid for selling secrets! Read on to find out how!

Stuff You'll Need
- UV marker
- Four one-dollar bills
- UV light

Your Network
- Four friends to act as suspected spies

What You Do

1 Using the UV marker, mark one of the bills by drawing a pair of glasses on George Washington. This marked dollar will represent money paid to a spy for selling secret information.

2 Gather four friends into a room. Place your marked dollar in the center of the room and tell your friends that this dollar is payment for spy work. After you leave the room, one of your friends will play the role of the spy and pick up payment for her work.

3 Leave the three unmarked dollar bills in a stack in another part of the room. Each person who is *not* the spy should take one of these bills (after you leave the room). This way, everyone will have a dollar, and it'll be your job to use your *ultra*secret method to find out which friend took the spy money!

4 Leave the room, and your friends will take their dollars. They should let you know when they're done.

5 When you return to the room, claim that you will be able to catch the spy in the dark! Turn off the lights and have each friend show you the bill he or she took. Shine your UV light on each bill. When you find good ol' George wearing his glasses, you've caught your spy!

MORE FROM HEADQUARTERS

Try using the UV marker to mark items that belong to you, like your favorite books and magazines.

If they end up in the wrong hands, you'll be able to prove they're yours *ultra*-quick.

WHAT'S THE SECRET?

When you mark money using UV ink, the mark will be invisible in normal light. But just like the UV **spy dust**, the UV marker contains chemicals that will **fluoresce** when UV light is shined on them, making the ink visible.

SPYtales

UV ink and UV spy dust aren't the *only* substances that glow when UV light is shined on them. Some kinds of glue will fluoresce, too. In one spy case, glowing glue gave **counterspies** the break they needed!

When counterspies checked the home of a suspected Russian spy operating in West Germany, one of the devices they used was a UV light. When they shined the light on a dish of walnuts, they were surprised to find that one of the walnuts glowed along its edge. Upon closer inspection, the counterspies discovered that the walnut had been cracked open, and glue had been used to reseal it. When the walnut was reopened, counterspies found **cipher** sheets used for enciphering and deciphering secret messages.

Glowing edge

This walnut was found inside a Russian spy's apartment. Inside is a pad of one-time cipher sheets—a complex cipher system in which the same cipher is never used twice! You'll learn more about this later on in your Spy University training.

#4 OPERATION Spy PRINT

Greasy fingerprints might not be welcome on windows, but they sure are a **counterspy**'s best friend! If a fingerprint is found on a packet of documents left in a **dead drop** by a spy, it might be just the evidence a counterspy needs to pin down the spy's identity.

In this operation, you'll learn how to find and collect fingerprints by *dusting* for them. And no, this is not housekeeping! So, if you want to learn some *handy* tricks for picking up fingerprints, check out this operation!

Stuff You'll Need

- Freshly washed (and dried) drinking glass
- Gloves
- Newspaper
- Baby powder
- 👓 Magnifying glass
- Clear tape
- Black construction paper
- 👓 Fingerprint cards (from your *Trainee Kit*)

Your Network

- Three or more friends (preferably ones whose fingerprint records you have already collected)

What You Do

Part 1: Printing your Paws

In this part of the operation, you'll practice making and collecting your own fingerprints. These kinds of fingerprints are called **latent fingerprints**. They're made when the natural oils of your skin are left behind on a surface you touch with your finger. So, get ready to leave your mark—and then pick it up again!

1 Find a smooth drinking glass that's clean and dry—fresh from the dishwasher, if possible. If necessary, wash the glass and dry it with a towel, being careful to avoid touching the glass while you're drying it (hold the glass with the towel).

19

2 Put a glove on one hand. This is the hand you'll use to pick up your freshly washed glass.

3 Now you're going to make a thumbprint on the glass. Since latent fingerprints are made by natural skin oils, you'll get a better print if your thumb is extra oily. So, rub your thumb along the side of your nose or through your hair. Those are both places where your body naturally produces oils.

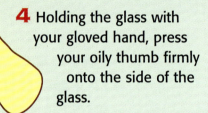

4 Holding the glass with your gloved hand, press your oily thumb firmly onto the side of the glass.

5 Remove your thumb and look at the print you left behind. Tilt the glass so you can see the print in the light. How much detail can you make out?

6 Now you're going to dust your print so you can examine it more easily. Spread out a newspaper and lay the glass on top of it, on its side, with the thumbprint facing up.

7 Sprinkle the baby powder over the thumbprint.

8 Gently shake the powder off the glass. Most of the powder will fall away, but some of it will stick to the thumbprint. Blow gently on the print to remove any extra powder.

9 Examine the print carefully. Use your magnifying glass to get a closer look. Can you see the pattern of your thumbprint more clearly now?

10 Now it's time to lift your print from the glass. Tear off a piece of clear tape that's about 2 inches (5 cm) long. Carefully place the sticky side of the tape over your powdered thumbprint. Make sure that the tape lands evenly and sticks firmly to the glass. Smooth the tape down with your finger.

11 Carefully lift the tape off the glass. The thumbprint should stick to the tape.

12 Place the sticky side of the tape onto the black construction paper.

13 Look at the fingerprint on the paper using your magnifying glass. Can you recognize your fingerprint type? The chart on the next page shows the common types, as you learned in your *Trainee Handbook*.

FINGERPRINT TYPES

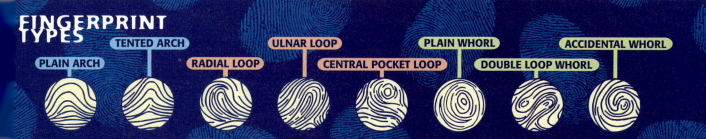

PLAIN ARCH · TENTED ARCH · RADIAL LOOP · ULNAR LOOP · CENTRAL POCKET LOOP · PLAIN WHORL · DOUBLE LOOP WHORL · ACCIDENTAL WHORL

14 Compare the print you collected to the thumbprint you made on your fingerprint record card from your *Trainee Kit*. Would you be able to match the two prints?

15 Repeat this process with your other fingers, using parts of the glass that are still clean.

Note: Don't be discouraged if you have a difficult time lifting fingerprints at first. It takes practice, and the more times you do it, the better results you'll get!

PART 2: CATCH THE SPY!

Now's your chance to put your fingerprint-dusting skills to the test! Just find three (or more) friends who are willing to be your suspects!

1 First, you need to get fingerprint records for each of your friends. In **Operation Dirty Fingers** from your *Trainee Handbook*, you created fingerprint records for three friends. If you're working with the same friends whose records you collected back then, all the better. Otherwise, make new fingerprint records following the steps outlined in your handbook.

2 Gather several friends in a room. Place a clean glass in front of them. Tell them that after you leave, one of them should pick up the glass once and set it down.

3 Return to the room, and put on *both* gloves (so you don't touch the glass at all).

4 Sprinkle the surface of the glass with baby powder and gently shake the glass to reveal where the fingerprints are. Blow off the extra powder. You'll most likely see more than just finger*tips* on the glass—the lower sections of your suspect's fingers will probably also show up.

5 Lift the fingerprints from the glass, following steps 10 through 12 from Part 1. Focus on lifting the prints made by the finger*tips*, not the lower parts of the fingers.

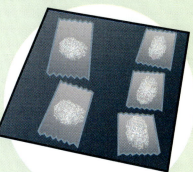

SPYtales

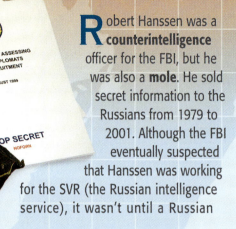

Robert Hanssen was a **counterintelligence** officer for the FBI, but he was also a **mole**. He sold secret information to the Russians from 1979 to 2001. Although the FBI eventually suspected that Hanssen was working for the SVR (the Russian intelligence service), it wasn't until a Russian **defector** (a former Russian intelligence officer who had fled to the United States) brought a plastic garbage bag to the FBI that they started to close in on Hanssen. When the FBI dusted the garbage bag for fingerprints, they found Hanssen's thumbprint. That one thumbprint turned out to be a key piece of evidence in the case against Hanssen, and it helped get him convicted. He is now spending the rest of his life in jail.

Robert Hanssen wrapped and taped his highly classified FBI documents inside black garbage bags before leaving them for the Russians to pick up. Hanssen's thumbprint was found on one of the bags—and that helped the FBI catch him.

6 Using your fingerprint records, identify who picked up the glass. Begin by identifying a main feature of each fingerprint. Does it have an arch, a loop, or a whorl? If you have a fingerprint with a loop, you only have to look for loop fingerprints on your records. Can you identify your spy? Take your best guess and ask your friends if you're right. If you have trouble, don't be discouraged—just keep practicing! As you learned in your *Trainee Handbook*, it's not easy to match fingerprints!

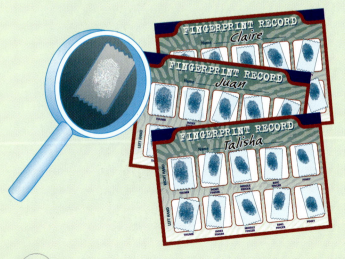

MORE FROM HEADQUARTERS

1 Try dusting for fingerprints on other smooth surfaces, like windows, mirrors, glazed ceramic items, or metal objects. Where do you collect the best fingerprints?

 2 Test your skills at matching fingerprints on the Spy University web site at **www.scholastic.com/spy**.

WHAT'S THE SECRET?

Unless you've just washed your hands, your fingers are sure to have some natural oils on them. Those oils make fingerprints not only on smooth surfaces, like the glass you worked with in this operation, but also on rougher surfaces like metal, paper, plastic, cardboard, wood, or even cloth!

The substance used to develop a latent fingerprint depends on where the fingerprint is found. Even on smooth surfaces, real counterspies wouldn't use baby powder. Instead, they would use fine black carbon powder (similar to the toner used in a copy machine) for latent prints on light-colored surfaces, and fine white aluminum powder or a chemical called lanconide for prints on dark-colored surfaces.

If the fingerprint is on a rougher surface, such as paper, cloth, wood, or plaster, counterspies will use chemical vapors to make the prints visible. Some of the chemicals used are iodine and ninhydrin. A fine mist of the chemical is sprayed on the surface where the latent print is suspected to be, and the chemical sticks to the fingerprint, making it visible.

A counterspy's fingerprint detection kit.

SPYquest

(continued from page 9)

After school, you go over to Beth's house, and she takes you up to her room. She opens the drawer next to her bed and shows you where she keeps her diary. The first thing you realize is that she doesn't have very good security. She should have done a better job of hiding something with valuable information like a diary!

"I know," Beth says. "From now on, I'm locking it up!"

You carefully take the diary out of the drawer, spread out some newspaper, and begin to dust the diary with baby powder. You're disappointed to find that the cloth cover doesn't show any fingerprints because the surface is too rough and irregular. But on the diary's brass latch, the powder reveals a good fingerprint. You use tape to transfer the print to a piece of black paper, then begin to examine it with your magnifying glass.

You'll have to collect the suspects' fingerprints somehow, and you start thinking of clever ways to do this, like offering each person a glass of water and taking prints from the glass. But first you have to make sure the print isn't Beth's.

You look at your samples of Beth's prints, and sure enough, the print is hers. Too bad!

■ This was a dead end. Turn back and try again.

#5 OPERATION READ MY Lips

Fingerprints aren't the only evidence a spy can leave behind. If the spy took a drink from a glass, her lip print might have been left behind, too. How's *that* going to help in a **counterspy**'s investigation? Well, just like fingerprints, lip prints are unique to each person. The grooves and patterns in a lip print can be used to trace the print back to its maker. So, if you want to learn how to read some *groovy* lips, read on!

Stuff You'll Need
- Lipstick
- Paper
- Pen or pencil
- Magnifying glass

Your Network
- Three friends (probably girls) to make lip prints

What You Do
Part 1: Lip and Learn!

1 First of all, you'll need to collect some lip prints to analyze, so get some of your friends to help you out. Since this involves wearing lipstick, you'll probably have an easier time recruiting girl volunteers! (You can collect your own lip print, too.)

2 Have each friend apply lipstick.

3 Have each friend "kiss" a piece of paper by placing the paper on a hard surface and pressing her lips to it. When she's finished making the print, she should write her name on the paper and hand it to you.

4 Look at the lip print with your magnifying glass. Do you see grooves in the lip surface? Those grooves are the focus of lip print analysis. The most common lip groove types are branching grooves, diamond grooves, rectangular grooves, long vertical grooves, and short vertical grooves. Lips are normally a combination of two or more of these patterns.

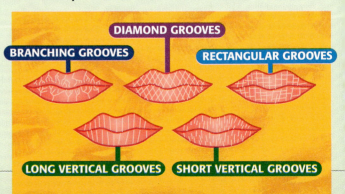

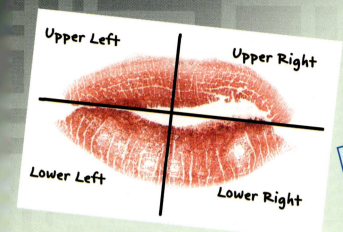

friends. Divide the mystery print into four sections, and use the chart you made to help with your analysis. Can you identify who made the print? The mystery print might not look *exactly* like one of your samples (because of differences in the way the lips were pressed to the paper), but can you find one sample that has the *most* similar characteristics?

5 To better analyze the lip print, divide it into four sections: upper left, upper right, lower left, and lower right.

6 Look at the groove patterns in each of the four areas. Which type (or types) of grooves do you see *most* in each area? Create a chart like the one below to keep track of your findings.

Name	Upper Left	Upper Right	Lower Left	Lower Right
Monique	Rectangular grooves	Rectangular grooves	Long vertical grooves. Some branching grooves on far left side	Long vertical grooves. Some branching grooves on far right side
Julia	Branching grooves	Branching grooves	Long vertical grooves, branching at bottom	Long vertical grooves, branching at bottom
Lisa	Long vertical grooves, tiny branches at top	Long vertical grooves, tiny branches at top	Long vertical grooves, tiny branches at bottom	Long vertical grooves, tiny branches at bottom

PART 2: MYSTERY LIPS

Now that you've analyzed four different lip prints, see if you can use your skills to identify the maker of a mystery print!

1 Leave the room and have one of your friends make a separate lip print on a new piece of paper.

2 Return to the room and examine the new lip print with your magnifying glass. Compare the print to the samples you collected from your

MORE FROM HEADQUARTERS

1 Try lifting a lipstick lip print from a glass. You can do this by placing a piece of tape over the lipstick mark and lifting the tape. Some of the lipstick will come away with the tape. You can then place the tape on a piece of white paper to get a better look at the print.

2 An enemy spy has been meeting with a **mole** in your network! You find their last meeting place, and you discover a glass with a lip print on it! See if you can match the lip print you found with one of the five shown below. Can you figure out who's the mole? You can check your answer on page 48.

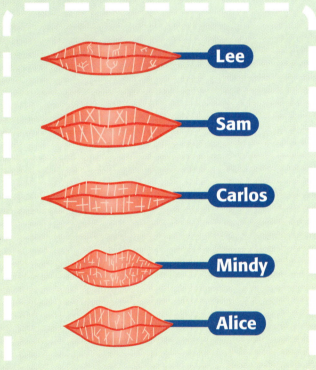

WHAT'S THE SECRET?

The study of lip prints is called **cheiloscopy** (not exactly a word that rolls off your lips, huh?). Each person has a unique set of lip prints, and they don't change over time. Because of this, lip prints can be used to identify the person who left the print behind.

Although they are less common than fingerprints, lip prints are often found on drinking glasses and cups, facial tissues, and even on letters. And just like fingerprints, it's possible to dust for lip prints, too, using the same methods that you used in **Operation Spy Print**. One problem with lip prints, though, is that they cannot be used in court trials, since cheiloscopy is still a very inexact science (as you might have discovered when you were trying to determine the maker of your mystery print!).

You might have also wondered what happens when lips are chapped. That can definitely make it tough to analyze a lip print. When lips are chapped, they get cracked and flaky, making it hard to see the natural groove patterns. As if lip print analysis wasn't hard enough already!

(continued from page 30)

You hold the envelope up to the light and notice that the smudge looks like some kind of greasy substance, like lip balm. Looking closer, you can see that the smudge has a lip print in it! Whoever submitted the information must have held the envelope in his or her mouth at some time, maybe because both hands were full.

You look carefully at the lip print using your magnifying glass, trying to see what the groove patterns look like, but the lip print is too smeared to help you out.

Later, you ask Beth which of her friends might wear lip balm.

"*All* of them," she says.

Oh, well.

■ This was a dead end. Turn back and try again.

East German Criminalists:
Super Spy Catchers

For many years after World War II (1939-1945), Germany was divided into two countries, East Germany and West Germany. In East Germany, counter-intelligence was very serious business. The East German government was always worried about being betrayed and was constantly on the lookout for spies.

Spy cases were investigated by the huge and powerful East German security service, the STASI. The STASI had some very highly trained counterspies called **criminalists**. Criminalists studied at Humboldt University in East Berlin, where they learned how to collect **trace evidence** (tiny clues like hair, dirt, or clothing fibers left behind by a spy). To conduct their investigations, the STASI criminalists used kits like the one on this page.

With the tools inside their kits, STASI criminalists could collect hair, fibers, and even liquid samples of body fluids. They could also create plaster and wax molds of any objects they wanted to study; they could measure, pry open, and examine things, and they could mark and document the evidence they gathered.

A criminalist kit, used by East German criminalists (highly trained counterspies) to investigate spy cases during the 1970s and 80s. The kit folded up to the size of a standard briefcase.

- RUBBER GLOVES
- SPONGE FOR COLLECTING LIQUIDS
- TWEEZERS
- WATERPROOF BAG TO HOLD DOCUMENTS
- CUP FOR MIXING PLASTER
- PLIERS
- HAMMER
- CHISEL
- BRUSH
- COMB FOR GATHERING HAIR AND FIBER SAMPLES
- TEST TUBES FOR STORING HAIR AND FIBER SAMPLES
- CANDLE THAT CAN BE MELTED TO MAKE WAX IMPRESSIONS
- GLASS BOTTLES FOR STORING SAMPLES
- TAPE MEASURE
- MAGNIFYING GLASS
- SPATULA FOR APPLYING PLASTER
- FLASHLIGHT

OPERATION INK LINK

#6

Suppose you've intercepted a coded note written in black ink. While you wait for code breakers to decode the message, are there any other clues? Absolutely. Every brand of pen uses different ink. Identify the ink, and you can identify the pen. If the spy owns such a pen, the noose begins to close around him! To learn how to use ink to link a spy to a message, try this operation!

Stuff You'll Need

- Basket-style coffee filter
- Ruler
- Pencil
- Scissors
- Masking tape
- Three different, water-soluble (not permanent), black felt-tip pens or markers
- Small cup
- Water
- Paper towel

Your Network

- A friend to play the part of the spy

What You Do

Part 1: Ink Blots

1 Flatten the basket-style coffee filter and lay it on the table in front of you.

2 Use the ruler and pencil to draw three 1-inch x 6-inch (2.5-cm x 15-cm) rectangles on the filter.

3 Use the scissors to cut out the rectangles. You should now have three strips of filter paper.

4 On each strip, draw a faint line with your pencil 1 inch (2.5 cm) from one end of the strip. Draw a second faint horizontal line 1½ inches (4 cm) above the first.

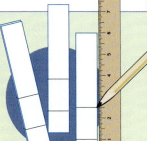

5 Assign a number to each of your black felt-tip pens. Label each pen by writing the number on a piece of masking tape and sticking the tape to the pen.

28

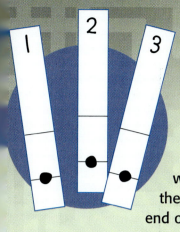

6 Using a different felt-tip pen each time, make a large dot in the center of the bottom line on each strip.

7 Use the pencil to write the number of the pen on the opposite end of the strip.

8 Place about ½ inch (1.5 cm) of water in the cup.

9 Choose one of the strips and lower it into the water, the end with the ink dot first. The ink dot should be about ½ inch (1.5 cm) above the surface of the water.

10 Watch the water as it moves up the strip. What happens when it reaches the ink dot?

11 Continue to hold the strip in place until the water has moved to the second pencil line.

12 Remove the strip from the water and place it on the paper towel.

13 Repeat steps 9 through 12 with the other two strips. Compare the ink patterns on the three strips. What do you notice?

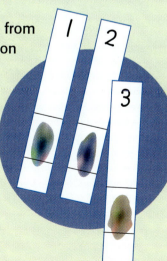

PART 2: INK-REDIBLE!

Do you think you can use what you observed in Part 1 to figure out which pen a spy used? Try this part of the operation to find out.

1 Prepare another filter strip, just like the three you prepared in Part 1.

2 Have a friend (who'll play the role of the pen-wielding spy) choose one of the three black pens and make a dot in the center of the bottom line on the strip. He should do this while you're out of the room, and he should not tell you which pen he used. That's for you to figure out!

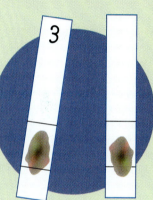

3 Return to the room, and follow steps 9 through 12 of Part 1 with the new strip. Look at the ink pattern that results, and compare it to the ink patterns on the three strips from Part 1. One of them should match. That's the pen your spy used!

MORE FROM HEADQUARTERS

Repeat the operation using different-colored felt-tip pens. Try green, purple, or brown. What do you notice about the patterns that develop from each ink color?

WHAT'S THE SECRET?

The process you've just learned is called **chromatography**. The black inks in the felt-tip pens you used in this operation are actually made up of many different dyes that have been mixed together. Chromatography is a way of analyzing the ink by separating the colors.

Here's how it works. First, the dyes dissolve in the water, and then the water moves up the coffee filter because of a process called *capillary attraction*. But capillary attraction doesn't *just* pull up the water; it *also* pulls up the dyes dissolved in the water. Because the different dyes that make up the black ink have different sizes and weights, they move upward at different speeds, with some moving faster (and farther) than others. This creates a pattern on the filter that can be used to identify the type of pen used to write a message.

But who writes messages on coffee filters? Fortunately, **counterspies** don't need the message to be written on a coffee filter in order to analyze the ink. Their laboratories can identify the type of pen used to write messages on normal paper, too.

SPYquest

(continued from page 9)

You go to the room where the school newspaper is published. When you enter, you find the student editor sitting behind a desk, reading the newspaper, just like everyone else.

"So," he asks, putting down the newspaper. "What can I do for you?"

"I'd like to find out who writes the 'Around School' column," you reply.

"So would a lot of people," he says. "But to tell you the truth, it's written by different people. We write some of the stuff ourselves; other stuff comes in from other kids at school, and sometimes we get things anonymously. Mr. Eckhert, our teacher sponsor, reviews the column before we can print it. He won't let us print anything that would really hurt anyone."

"What about the B.C.H. and S.L.L. information? Where did that come from?"

"It was an anonymous tip. I came in to school one morning and found it in an envelope that had been slipped under the door."

You think about that for a few seconds then ask, "Do you still have the note and the envelope?"

"I think so," the kid says and searches through a file.

"Yeah, here they are."

You look at the note with the information about Beth. It's been typed and printed out on what looks like a laser printer. You don't see any marks on the paper that would help you identify the sender, and at this point in your counterspy career, you don't have the right equipment to reveal invisible fingerprints on paper.

But the envelope the information came in is another story. The envelope is made of a lightweight paper, and the words "Around School" are handwritten on it in ink. There also appears to be a smudge in one corner. What might that be?

"Do you mind if I keep these?" you ask.

"Sure," the kid says. "Go ahead."

You turn and leave the room. Now you have another lead. There are two things you could do. One is to use ink chromatography and try to identify the kind of pen that was used to write the words on the envelope. The other is to investigate the smudge in the corner of the envelope.

- If you decide to use ink chromatography on the writing, turn to **page 33**.
- If you decide to investigate the smudge on the envelope, turn to **page 26**.

30

#7 OPERATION Bug Plant

Bugs are tiny devices that pick up sounds in a room and transmit them to another location. **Counterspies** use bugs to listen in on a suspected spy's conversations. However, if the spy spots the bug, the counterspy's investigation could be…squashed!

That's why bugs are designed to be cleverly hidden. As a counterspy, it's your job to *think* of those clever hiding places *and* manage to plant your bugs there without getting caught. Think you're up to the challenge? Then read on!

Stuff You'll Need
- Paper clips
- Colored paper
- Tape
- Pen or pencil

Your Network
- Several friends who want to be bugged

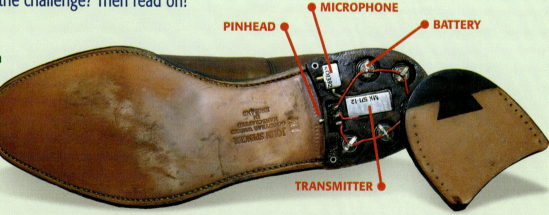

Here's a bug hidden inside the heel of a shoe! The device was activated by pulling out the small pinhead at the base of the heel.

PINHEAD • MICROPHONE • BATTERY • TRANSMITTER

What You Do

1 Have each of your friends use a paper clip, a small piece of colored paper, and tape to make one bug each. Each person's bug should be unique. To make sure you'll be able to tell the bugs apart, label them by writing the owner's initials on the paper part of the bug.

❶ PAPER CLIP
❷ TAPE
❸ PAPER
❹ OWNER'S INITIALS

2 Now you're going to play a game to see who's the greatest bug planter of them all!

The rules of the game are as follows:

- The game will last five days.

- The goal is to plant your bug on one of the other players without him realizing it. Since your goal is to "listen in" on the spy, the bug must be planted either on the person himself (very tricky!), on something he carries with him very often (like a backpack or a book), or at his desk. All other locations are off limits.

- In order to prove that your bug went undetected, you'll have to be able to retrieve it at the end of the game. So, make sure that you don't put your bug in a spot where you can't remove it later.

- One point is awarded for every twenty-four hours a bug goes undiscovered. Keep track of your own points.

- If you discover a bug, give it back to its owner as soon as possible. The owner may then replant the bug on another player the next day.

- At the end of five days, meet with your friends and compare points. The person with the most points is a Distinguished Bug Planter, First Class!

3 Since points are only awarded for bugs that go undiscovered for more than twenty-four hours, you'll need to think of very good hiding places. Consider using tape to stick your bug in unusual places (like between the pages of a notebook!). Here are some other examples of good hiding places:

- The gap in the binding of a hardcover book.

- Inside a retractable ballpoint pen. If you unscrew the pen, you can slide a bug inside the hollow pen barrel.

(continued from page 13)

You spread an even coating of UV spy dust on the floor near the drawer where Beth keeps her diary. Your trap is set!

Erica and Cassie arrive, and Beth suggests that you play hide-and-seek inside her house. The person who is "it" can start in her bedroom and count to a hundred while everyone else hides.

Once everyone has had a chance to be "it," you suggest watching some TV, mentioning that in order to go into the family room, everyone must take off their shoes. Once everyone's ready to go to the family room, you pretend that you have to go to the bathroom, but instead, you take out your UV light to check out the shoes.

Turning off the lights, you shine your UV light on the shoes. They're all glowing! Even yours and Beth's. It looks like the area you dusted was too big and the UV dust got on everyone's shoes.

- This was a dead end. Turn back and try again.

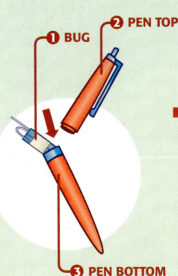

- Under the insole of a shoe.

What other hiding places can you think of? Be creative and rack up those points!

4 Don't forget to keep up your own security by sweeping for bugs that could be planted on you! Check all the places described above (and then some!) at least once a day. And be sure to watch your friends carefully when they're near your stuff!

More from Headquarters

Now try a second round of the game. This time, everyone can make *several* identical bugs (anywhere from three to five is a good number). All the other rules are the same, only now you have the chance to earn a ton of points, since you have more bugs to plant. Try to think of as many different hiding places as you can, and make sure to do a sweep of all the places where someone could have planted a bug on you!

At the end of five days, see who is the Master Bug Planter of your network.

What's the Secret?

The key to successful bug planting is not arousing your **target**'s suspicion. The best way is to plant the bug when your target is out of the room, but bugs can also be "planted" by hiding them in pens or books that are then given to the target or "accidentally" left behind during a visit to the target's home or office. In the spy world, this technique is called a **quick plant**.

Counterspies don't just *plant* bugs, though. Just as you did in this operation, real counterspies also have to be on the lookout for bugs planted on *their* turf by enemy spies. To control the spread of bugs, intelligence agencies routinely "sweep" their offices using devices that detect radio signals. After they detect and locate the bug, they look for people who may have been in the office and could have planted the bug. This is often the first step in locating a **mole** in the agency.

(continued from page 30)

You take the envelope and cut a strip from it, making sure that the ink writing is about an inch from the bottom of the strip. You fill a glass with water, then take one strip and hold it so that the bottom of it is in the water. You wait. After the water has climbed up the strip, you take the strip out of the water and lay it on a paper towel to dry.

A few minutes later, Beth arrives with the samples you asked her to collect earlier. She hands over ink samples from four black pens, each taken from a friend who was in her room recently.

"They didn't suspect a thing," Beth says. "I just asked to borrow their pens for a second!"

You soak each of Beth's strips in water. You look at the ink patterns, and you know you're onto something. You can't be certain, but the kind of pen used to write on the front of the envelope is the same kind that two of Beth's friends, Erica and Cassie, own. But maybe other kids in the school use the same kind of pen. How can you be sure that Erica and Cassie are the culprits?

One way would be to set some kind of a trap. You could leave Beth's diary out again and see who goes to get it. The other option would be to conduct surveillance on the two people you suspect and see if you can find out anything that way.

- If you decide to set a trap with Beth's diary, turn to **page 13**.
- If you decide to conduct surveillance, turn to **page 36**.

OPERATION #8: Catch the Wave

Radio waves are not just for music—they're also great for spy communication. Spies can use portable radio transmitters to send coded messages from secret locations. Even if **counterspies** intercept the transmissions, they'll still have to break the code, and the spy's location will remain unknown…or will it? Try this operation to find out how to catch a radio wave— *and* the spy who sent it!

Stuff You'll Need
- Ruler
- Pencil

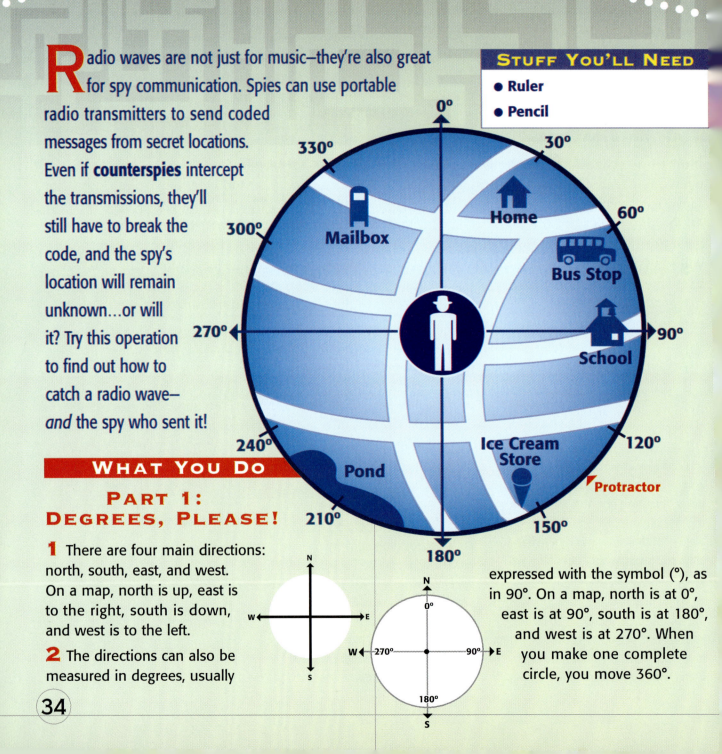

What You Do

Part 1: Degrees, Please!

1 There are four main directions: north, south, east, and west. On a map, north is up, east is to the right, south is down, and west is to the left.

2 The directions can also be measured in degrees, usually expressed with the symbol (°), as in 90°. On a map, north is at 0°, east is at 90°, south is at 180°, and west is at 270°. When you make one complete circle, you move 360°.

3 You can use an instrument called a protractor to measure degrees. For example, using the 360° protractor shown on page 34, you can see that the school is at 90°, or exactly east of you. Can you find what's located in each of the following directions? You can check your answers on page 48.

    a. **30°**   b. **60°**   c. **150°**   d. **330°**

Part 2: X Marks the Spot!

Now that you know how to use a protractor, let's catch a spy. You know that the spy will be transmitting a secret message tonight at 2200 hours (that's 10:00 p.m. in non-spy time!) from somewhere in the city, and you have your counterintelligence team ready for action. Agents Delta and Echo have moved to their locations on opposite sides of the city and turned on their radio receivers.

1 At 2200 hours, Agents Delta and Echo receive the spy's radio signal and call in the following directions.

- Agent Delta reports a signal at 30° from his location.
- Agent Echo reports a signal at 300° from her location.

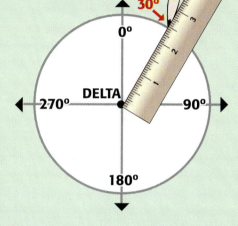

2 To locate the spy's radio, use your ruler to draw a pencil line from Delta's location through the 30° mark on Delta's protractor. Draw the line all the way across the map. The radio is located somewhere along that line. But where? That's where the information from Agent Echo comes in.

3 Using your ruler, draw a second pencil line from Echo's location through the 300° mark on Echo's protractor. Draw the line all the way across the map.

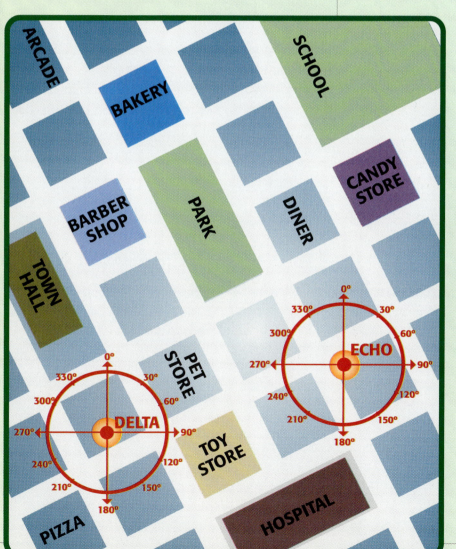

The spy's radio is located where Echo's line crosses Delta's line (X marks the spot!).

You now know where to find the spy! So, hurry over to page 48, where you can check your answer and catch that spy!

More from Headquarters

Agents Delta and Echo are hot on the trail of another spy! This time, they report the following information:

- Agent Delta reports a signal at 30° from his location.
- Agent Echo reports a signal at 0° from her location.

Can you find the spy's location? You can check your answer on page 48!

What's the Secret?

The method you've just learned is called **triangulation**. If any two points of a triangle are known (in this case, the locations of your two agents), the third can be located using this technique. Sailors have used triangulation for years to determine their locations at sea. The ship's navigator takes sightings of landmarks like lighthouses, islands, or even stars. Using a protractor and a good map, he can figure out the ship's location in relation to the landmarks. During World War II (1939–1945), the Germans used radio receivers and triangulation to locate the radio transmitters of resistance fighters.

Nowadays, a spy's *cell phone* can be used to pinpoint his location. The cell phone can be located by finding where the signal is in relation to the communication towers that pick up the signal and transmit it.

(continued from page 33)

You decide to conduct surveillance to keep an eye on the suspects. You begin with Erica. You watch her from around the corner during lunch as she whispers to some friends, but you can't hear what she's saying. You hide behind a tree after school and watch her walk the other way up the street. After a while, it becomes clear you're not getting anywhere this way, so you decide on a new tactic. You arrange to get Erica and Cassie together at Beth's house.

You talk to Beth about setting up surveillance in her house, and Beth invites both Cassie and Erica over to do homework the next day after school. As you watch secretly from the dining room, the girls begin to work. They talk about school, and Cassie and Erica are both full of gossip.

At one point, Cassie says she needs to use the bathroom and leaves. You quietly slip over to a new hiding place in the living room, where you have a view of the bathroom door. You watch as Cassie comes out to see if she goes up the stairs to Beth's room, but instead, she looks straight at you!

"What are *you* doing here?" she asks.

Oh, my. You have some explaining to do! Better think fast!

- That sure was a dead end! Turn back and try again!

#9

OPERATION Spies on Wheels

Guess what, **counterspy**? Now's your chance to learn how to follow a spy in a car! Never driven a car? Don't have a driver's license yet? That's all right. You can still learn the basics of vehicle **surveillance** by playing a game of *Spies on Wheels* (a board game you'll find on pages 40 and 41). So, start your engines, and get ready to hit the road!

Stuff You'll Need
- The game board on pages 40 and 41
- Five pennies
- One dime
- Pencil

Your Network
- A friend to play the game with you

What You Do

Part 1: Get Ready

Looking forward to getting behind the wheel? Well, here are the keys to your brand-new… penny! That's right—in the game of *Spies on Wheels*, you'll be driving coins around the streets of Spyville. This part of the operation will show you how to maneuver your fleet of vehicles for the best results!

1 In this game, the dime represents the **target** vehicle (driven by a suspected spy), and the pennies represent the **surveillance** vehicles (driven by counterspies). Your friend will control the target vehicle, and you'll control the five surveillance vehicles.

2 The surveillance team will use a technique called the Floating Box. A Floating Box can involve anywhere from three to twenty vehicles. In this case, we've used five. The cars are arranged as shown below.

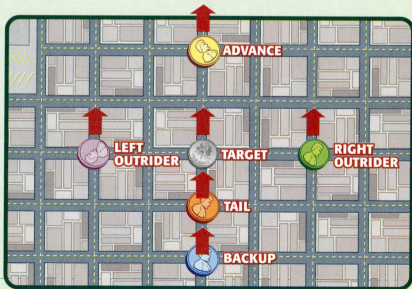

Each car has a different role:

Tail: This vehicle follows behind the target vehicle. Sometimes the tail vehicle will be *directly* behind the target, and other times it might let one or two cars get between itself and the target so that the target doesn't always see the same car behind it. The tail's main job is to always keep the target in sight and to tell the other members of the team what the target is doing.

Backup: This vehicle occasionally takes over for the tail vehicle. If the tail vehicle remains behind the target for too long, the target is likely to see it and get suspicious. That's why it's good for the tail and the backup to switch places from time to time.

Advance: This vehicle lets the rest of the team know what's ahead on the route. It can tell the team if there are obstacles, road construction, or heavy traffic that might cause the target vehicle to change direction.

Outriders: These vehicles stay on either side of the target. They also play a key role when the target vehicle changes direction, since they will have to take over the roles of the tail vehicle and the advance.

3 So, how does the Floating Box move? When the target moves in one direction, the box just *floats* along with it. When the target turns a *corner*, however, the surveillance cars change positions as shown below.

4 Keep the Floating Box technique in mind as you play *Spies on Wheels*. It'll help you keep your target right where you want him!

When the target makes a left turn, the Floating Box rearranges itself as shown here.

ADVANCE becomes OUTRIDER

LEFT OUTRIDER becomes ADVANCE

TARGET turns left

RIGHT OUTRIDER becomes TAIL

TAIL becomes BACKUP

BACKUP becomes OUTRIDER

Part 2: Get Set!

Now it's time to learn how to play the game. First, turn the page and look at the game board. Then turn back here to learn the rules. Here are the basics:

- Your goal is to have as many cars as possible surrounding your target at the end of the game.
- Your target's goal is to lose as many surveillance cars as he can before the end of the game.

These are the rules:

- The target goes first, moving one block (to the next intersection). Then the surveillance cars move one block each.
- Either player may choose *not* to move a car during a turn.
- If the target moves onto the same space as a surveillance car, that surveillance car *must* be moved during the surveillance team's next turn. A surveillance car cannot move onto the same spot as the target.
- If a car lands on one of the spaces marked Ø, ⊕, or +2, follow the instructions for that space immediately:
  - Ø The player removes any *one* surveillance car from the board. (The surveillance cars must avoid the Ø spots!)
  - ⊕ The player adds *one* surveillance car to the board (but only if at least one car has already been removed). The car can be placed at any intersection. (The target must avoid the ⊕ spots.)
  - +2 The car advances two more blocks.
- Each player can only use the Ø and ⊕ spaces once. The +2 spaces can be reused as often as you want.
- After each player has moved ten times, the game is over.

Now count up your points. You get one point for each surveillance car that has not lost the target car. A surveillance car is considered "lost" if it's more than two blocks away from the target. How'd you do? Check your rank on the chart below.

POINTS	RANK
5 points	Road Ruler
4 points	Wheel Wonder
3 points	Street Smartie
2 points	Decent Driver
1 point	Basic Beginner
0 points	Try again!

More from Headquarters

Now switch roles with your friend and play the game as the target. How many of your friend's surveillance cars can you lose?

What's the Secret?

In this operation, you used pennies to represent **counterintelligence** vehicles. In reality, though, counterspies would never use identical vehicles. The counterspies would vary the make, model, color, and style of the vehicles they used to ensure that the target did not become alarmed by seeing the same car again and again.

Counterspies can also use tracking devices to keep tabs on a spy's car. The devices can be attached to the underside of the car, and they'll send out radio signals that counterspies can monitor.

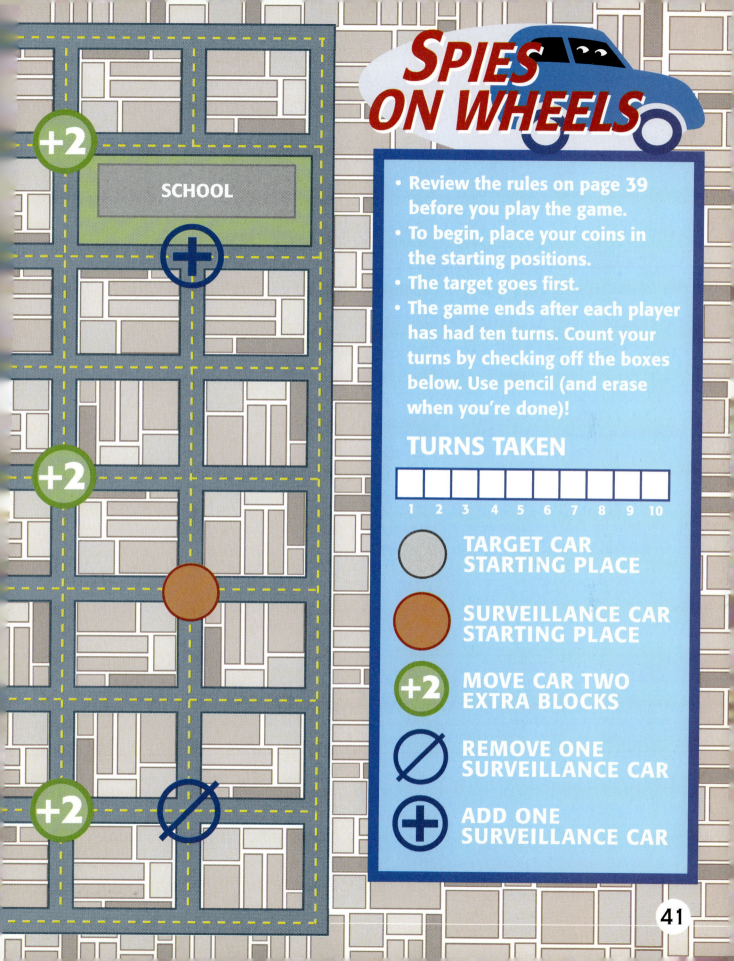

OPERATION

#10

Having trouble reading the title? You'll have better luck after you finish this operation—*if* you succeed at breaking the code, of course! For a **counterspy**, breaking a spy's coded messages can crack a case wide open. That's why you've got to be ready to face whatever code comes your way. This operation may take some time, but see it through!

Stuff You'll Need
- Pencil and paper

What You Do

Suppose you discovered the following message:

How would you go about trying to break the code?

1 Begin by looking at the symbols used in the code. Do you notice any similarities or patterns? Maybe you can find a clue that will help you decode the message.

2 On a blank piece of paper, create a chart listing each symbol that's used in the message.

3 Count the number of times each symbol appears in the message and note the total number of appearances in the right column.

4 Which symbol is used the most of all? There's a good chance that symbol represents the letter E, the most commonly used letter in the English language. Write the letter E below the most common symbol each time it appears (this is just a guess, but since it's an *educated* guess, hopefully it'll pay off!).

5 Look at the other symbols that appear frequently. They might represent the other most commonly used letters in English. After **E**, the most commonly used letters are **T**, **A**, **O**, **N**, **I**, **R**, and **S**. See if you can figure out if any of the commonly used symbols might represent those letters.

6 Use other code-breaking techniques to help you.

- **Look for one-letter words.** Can you guess what they are?

- **Look for two-letter words.** There are only a few two-letter words in English—like *of*, *to*, *in*, *is*, *it*, *be*, *by*, *he*, *as*, *on*, *at*, *or*, *an*, *so*, *if*, and *no*.

7 When you think you have a few symbols decoded, make a chart of the alphabet in A-to-Z order. Write each symbol you know next to the letter it represents. Do you recognize a pattern? Give yourself some time! Once you've recognized the pattern, you can start to fill in the code symbols for the other letters of the alphabet. You can find the complete solution on page 48.

More from Headquarters

On the Spy University web site (**www.scholastic.com/spy**), you can create and print out messages in this code!

What's the Secret?

Breaking codes is a lot like doing crossword puzzles or playing hangman. You start with a few letters, then you can fill in a whole word! You just have to use your knowledge of language (and some good guesswork!) to fill in the blanks.

(continued from page 13)

You figure that a UV trap on the diary itself is probably the best way to catch the mole. You brush UV spy dust on the outside of the diary and you're ready to go.

You have Beth invite Erica and Cassie over to her house. Beth suggests that you all play hide-and-seek inside the house. The person who is "it" will start in Beth's bedroom and count to a hundred while everyone else hides.

By the end of the game, everyone has had a chance to be "it," which means everyone got to be alone in the bedroom with the diary. You gather everyone together and ask them to hold out their hands. They're a bit confused, but they do it anyway. You turn on your UV light and begin to shine it on everyone's hands. Cassie's hands are clean! When you get to Erica, though, her fingers glow green from the powder they touched when she picked up Beth's diary. You explain to Erica what this means.

"Why did you do it?" you ask.

She looks at Beth. "It was for your own good," she says. "I accidentally found your diary when you sent me up to your room to get the book you'd borrowed from me. I read that you liked Steven and waited for you to do something about it. But you didn't. And I was worried you'd never do anything about it. I know that Steven likes you, too, but he's been waiting for you to make the first move. He could wind up waiting forever—I know you. I thought that the column might give the romance a little nudge. Don't be mad."

"Erica is right," Cassie adds. "I know it wasn't right to look at Beth's diary, but she was only trying to help."

You look at Beth and Erica. Beth doesn't say anything for a moment, then asks, "Do you really think Steven likes me?"

Erica and Cassie look at each other and smile. "We're sure of that."

With that, everyone laughs.

Well, the case is closed. And tomorrow, Beth says she's going to talk to Steven… just to see what happens.

- **Congratulations! Quest accomplished!**

43

Aldrich Ames, a mole inside the CIA, spied for the Russians from 1985 to 1994. He betrayed his country for money.

Aldrich Ames, CIA MOLE

It's one thing to spy *for* your country—and quite another to spy *against* it. That's when a spy becomes a traitor, betraying the trust of the people who think he's on their side.

What would make someone betray his own country? There are lots of reasons—everything from strong political beliefs to personal grudges. But the strongest motivation for becoming a spy is *money*, plain and simple. Other countries will pay spies big bucks for the secrets they hand over, and for some people, all that money is just too hard to resist.

That's exactly what happened in the case of Aldrich Ames, a **mole** inside the CIA, who spied for the Russians from 1985 to 1994.

Aldrich Ames made an early entrance into the spy field. His father, Carleton Ames, worked for the CIA, and Aldrich wanted to follow in his footsteps. Carleton helped Aldrich get a summer job with the CIA when he was sixteen. Then, after he flunked out of college in 1962, Ames got his first job with the CIA as a low-level clerk. Ames finished college while working at the agency and applied for the CIA's Career Trainee Program. He became a CIA officer in 1968.

As a CIA officer, Ames worked in the Soviet division, recruiting and handling Russian spies. Then, in 1983, Ames was given a very important job: He became the Soviet branch chief of the CIA's **counterintelligence** group. In this position, Ames was responsible for reviewing the cases of Russians who had been recruited as CIA agents and deciding whether or not they were trustworthy. Ames had access to information on all the Russians who were secretly working for the CIA. That was a lot of very sensitive—and *valuable*—information. And Ames knew it.

By 1985, Ames was ready to cash in on the CIA's secrets. He was deep in debt. He had gone through a costly divorce from his first wife, and he had a new wife, Rosario, who had expensive tastes. He needed money—and he knew he could get it by selling CIA secrets to the Russians.

Ames began by delivering a letter to the Soviet embassy in Washington, D.C., listing a few Russians who were secretly working for the United States. As a twenty-three-year veteran of the CIA, Ames knew what could happen to the men he betrayed, but he did it anyway. For this information, Ames was paid $50,000.

During the next nine years, Ames revealed more than a hundred secret operations and betrayed more than thirty Russians who were working with the CIA and FBI. At least ten of the spies were executed after their identities were revealed. By the time Ames was caught in 1994, the Soviet Union had funneled almost $2.7 million to him. That made him the highest-paid spy in history!

The CIA initially believed the traitor was Edward Lee Howard, a former CIA officer who **defected** (or fled) to the Soviet Union in 1985. However, some of the Russians who had been betrayed were unknown to Howard. That meant there had to be *another* mole inside the CIA. After an examination of the names of CIA officers who had knowledge of the Russian agents who were betrayed, a short list of possible moles was assembled.

Ames made a chalk mark on this mailbox, code-name SMILE, to signal his Russian handlers that he was ready to deliver information.

After each name was studied, the spending habits of one man, Aldrich Ames, stood out. He was living a grand lifestyle and spending well beyond his income. Ames had bought a $540,000 house with cash, wore designer clothes, and drove a luxury car (a fancy Jaguar) to work at the CIA. His new wife, Rosario, completely refurnished their entire house, sparing no expense.

This Post-it note, recovered from Ames's trash, contained a message from Ames to his Russian handlers.

Ames told his CIA colleagues that his wealth came from his wife's family in Colombia. Ames told his wife (who knew her family wasn't wealthy) that the money came from a friend named "Robert" in Chicago, whom Ames was helping with business investments. In 1992, Rosario discovered what her husband was *really* up to, and she began supporting him in his spy work. The CIA, however, had a tougher time exposing Ames's lies. And so Ames managed to stay in business as a Soviet spy for almost a decade.

During this time, the CIA went down many dead ends in its search for the mole. Ames even passed *two* lie detector tests while he was spying for the Russians. But finally, the CIA's mole hunters started to close in on Ames.

Jean Vertefeuille, a quiet older woman who had worked for the CIA for thirty-two years, headed the mole hunt team. Vertefeuille's team interviewed many CIA officers who had access to the information that was provided to the Russians. One question Vertefeuille asked was, "If you were going to volunteer to give information to the Soviet government, how would you do it?" When Ames was asked this question, he became flustered and struggled to answer it, while the other interviewees simply described how they would go about contacting the Russians. This made Ames seem guiltier than ever.

The CIA took a closer look at Ames's wealth, and they found that large sums of money were being deposited into Ames's bank accounts from unknown sources. They also found that several bank deposits made in 1985 and 1986

Ames's arrest on February 21, 1994. His Jaguar was surrounded by FBI vehicles.